ISLE OF MAN RAILWAY JOURNEY

Steam days in colour

Tom Heavyside

Series editor Vic Mitchell

MP Middleton Press

Front cover: The headquarters of the Isle of Man Railway is at Douglas. No.11 Maitland *leaves for Port Erin on 26th April 2001. (T.Heavyside)*

Back cover upper: No trains have run to Peel or Ramsey since 1968. However the clock was turned back briefly on 22nd August 1998 when no.1 Sutherland *visited Peel. This was in connection with the celebrations held that year to commemorate the 125th anniversary of the opening of the Isle of Man Railway in 1873. Peel Castle on St Patrick's Isle is in the view, on the other side of the harbour. (T.Heavyside)*

Back cover lower: Services first began between Douglas, Castletown and Port Erin in 1874. No.8 Fenella *arrives at Castletown from Douglas on 24th October 2003. (T.Heavyside)*

ACKNOWLEDGEMENTS

In respect of the early images I am much indebted to photographers who had the foresight to use colour film from the 1960s. Their work is credited individually. My sincere thanks is due also to Paul Abell, Paul Chancellor, Mike Taylor, and the staff at the Manx Museum Library in Douglas for invaluable help. The copies of postage stamps are included by kind permission of the Isle of Man Post Office. The map, track plans and gradient profiles are by the late Roger Hateley, and tribute should be paid to his outstanding work, not only in this book but also in the preceding four volumes on the Isle of Man railways published by Middleton Press.

Published March 2017

ISBN 978 1 910356 02 9

© *Middleton Press, 2017*

Production Editor Deborah Esher
Design Cassandra Morgan
Cover design Matthew Esher

Published by
> *Middleton Press*
> *Easebourne Lane*
> *Midhurst*
> *West Sussex*
> *GU29 9AZ*
Tel: 01730 813169
Email: info@middletonpress.co.uk
www.middletonpress.co.uk

Printed and bound by CPI Group (UK) Ltd, Croydon, CR0 4YY

CONTENTS

INDEX

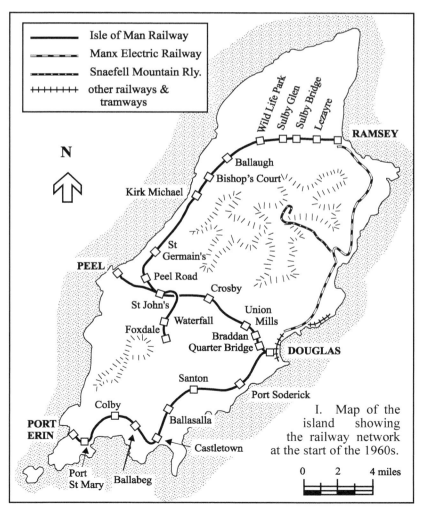

I. Map of the island showing the railway network at the start of the 1960s.

GEOGRAPHICAL SETTING

The Isle of Man, encircled by the Irish Sea, is situated 30 miles west of the nearest point on the Cumbrian coast, 45 miles north of Anglesey, 33 miles east of Northern Ireland and 18 miles south of Scotland. The island covers an area of approximately 227 square miles. From its northern extremity to the southern tip is a distance of 30 miles while the western and eastern coasts are never more than 10 miles apart.

The landscape in the north of the island is dominated by some high mountains, the tallest being Snaefell standing 2036ft above sea level. In the south, South Barrule at an altitude of 1586ft overlooks a less extensive but equally impressive range of mountains. Between the Northern Upland and Southern Upland Massifs is the narrow Central Valley.

Douglas is the capital and main port of the island. It lies on the eastern seaboard where the combined waters of the Dhoo and Glass rivers flow into the Irish Sea. The Douglas to Peel railway utilised the floor of the Central Valley, first keeping close to the meandering River Dhoo and, from just beyond Crosby, the River Greeba (a tributary of the Dhoo). The summit of the line was near Ballacurry crossing at a mere 185ft above sea level, from where it descended to St John's. The rails then threaded the valley of the River Neb to Peel, the principal fishing port along the west coast.

The Foxdale branch started some 250yds west of St John's, and skirted round the north side of the main station before crossing above the line from Douglas. The route then climbed continuously along the valley of the Foxdale River before reaching the lead mining village of Foxdale itself.

From St John's, the line to Ramsey paralleled that to Peel for a short way before diverging northwards. Beyond St Germain's as far as Orrisdale (between Kirk Michael and Ballaugh) the railway never strayed very far away from the western coastline, before turning east. After Sulby, the track stayed close to the river of the same name that empties its waters into the Irish Sea at Ramsey, the largest town in the north. By this circuitous path the railway avoided the high ground of the Northern Upland Massif.

The southern limb of the railway to Port Erin climbs steeply from Douglas through the Eastern Coastal Plateau to Keristal, near Port Soderick, before descending to Ballasalla. The railway then continues to descend across the Plain of Malew to Castletown, the former capital of the island, and on to Port St Mary. The final three-quarters of a mile to Port Erin is across the peninsula that separates the southern and western coasts.

For the most part the rails were supported on an underlying stratum of Manx slate. The exceptions were a short section at Peel, laid on a sandstone foundation, and that from Ballasalla to Port St Mary which rests on a layer of carboniferous limestone.

HISTORICAL BACKGROUND

The Isle of Man Railway Co Ltd was registered on 19th December 1870. On the recommendation of Henry Vignoles a gauge of 3ft 0in was adopted. The line from Douglas to Peel opened on Tuesday 1st July 1873, services between Douglas and Port Erin commencing on Saturday 1st August 1874.

Originally the IoMR had intended to serve all the main towns on the island, but to the dismay of those living in the north, plans for a line to Ramsey were abandoned. Thus a separate company was formed, the Manx Northern Railway Co Ltd, to promote a line from Ramsey via Kirk Michael to St John's, where a connection was made with IoMR metals. Services started without fanfare on Tuesday 23rd September 1879.

The nominally independent Foxdale Railway Co Ltd was registered on 16th November 1882, but in fact was very closely allied to the Manx Northern, most of the FR directors also being on the board of the MNR. The branch from St John's to Foxdale, operated by the MNR from the outset, officially opened on Monday 16th August 1886. However, within five years, in July 1891, the FR had gone into liquidation, the MNR then continuing to work the line on behalf of the liquidator.

On 19th April 1905 both the Manx Northern and Foxdale railways ceased to exist when they were taken over by the IoMR. From then until the outbreak of World War II in 1939 the fortunes of the IoMR fluctuated widely, much depending on the popularity or otherwise of the island as a holiday destination. The total number of passengers carried (all lines) annually ranged from a record 1,609,155 in 1920 to a low of 603,676 in 1930. Meanwhile, from the late 1920s, the railway company also became the island's major bus operator outside Douglas.

The railway suffered mixed fortunes during World War II. While the tourist trade became virtually non-existent, much traffic was generated with the establishment of numerous training facilities for the armed forces and camps for interned enemy aliens. From 1940 the scheduled passenger services along the Foxdale branch were usually replaced by buses. However after peace had been restored in 1945 visitors again began to flock to the island in droves, the railway carrying no fewer than 1,535,256 passengers in 1947. Unfortunately this boom was short-lived and by 1959 the number of passengers carried had fallen to 996,878, the vast majority travelling during the summer season. In the main this was due to a significant decline in the popularity of the island as a holiday destination, along with an increase in private car ownership.

At the turn of the decade into the 1960s the railway generally was in a somewhat parlous state and, as an economy measure, the St John's to Peel line was closed from October 1960 for the winter period. In subsequent years services between St John's and Ramsey were withdrawn during the winter months, the Peel and Port Erin routes remaining open. With seemingly no end to the decline it came as little surprise when, with only four days notice, services across the whole network were suspended after Saturday 13th November 1965. Officially this was to enable urgent track maintenance work to be carried out.

In the event the railway remained dormant throughout 1966, before a dramatic turnaround came about following the intervention of the Marquess of Ailsa who negotiated a 21 year lease of the entire railway, but with a break clause after five years. Under this new regime Douglas station witnessed a grand ceremonial reopening of the Peel line on Saturday 3rd June 1967, trains to Ramsey commencing the next day. Services to Castletown started on Tuesday 11th July, trains being unable to continue further west due to a new gas main being laid alongside the trackbed towards Port Erin. After the summer peak period the railway again closed for the winter.

In 1968, the railway became known as the Isle of Man Steam Railway. On the 'south line' trains once more ran through to Port Erin, but regrettably in respect of the lines to Peel and Ramsey this proved their swansong, as at the end of that season both were abandoned. Passenger services between St John's and Ramsey were concluded on Friday 6th September and between Douglas and Peel the next day. After this there were just a few freight and empty stock movements.

From 1969, trading as the Isle of Man Victorian Steam Railway, and with financial assistance from the Manx Government, Ailsa concentrated his activities on the Port Erin route before at the end of 1971 exercising his option to terminate the lease. The assets then reverted to the Isle of Man Railway. With further Government aid the service between Douglas and Port Erin was maintained during the tourist season, but in 1975 was confined to the Port Erin-Castletown section. The next year trains from Port Erin terminated at Ballasalla, before services were restored to the full length of the line in 1977.

Meanwhile, in 1976, the Manx Government acquired the land previously utilised by the former routes to Peel and Ramsey, which for the most part can now be walked as official footpaths. Then, early in 1978, following a decision by Tynwald (the Manx Parliament), the remaining assets of the IoMR were purchased by the Government, with day to day matters administered by the already nationalised Manx Electric Railway Board. In 1983 the railways, along with the buses, became the responsibility of the newly created Isle of Man Passenger Transport Board. At the end of 1986 the Transport and Tourist boards were merged to form the Department of Tourism and Transport. Today the island's transport undertakings come under the umbrella of the Department of Infrastructure.

PASSENGER SERVICES

By the early 1960s, the days when Douglas station witnessed over 20 departures daily during high summer had long since passed. For instance, from Monday 7th July 1947, 12 trains left Douglas each weekday destined for Port Erin, plus one extra on Saturdays. A further 11 headed west from Douglas to St John's (with an additional service on Saturdays), where most divided into separate portions for Peel and Ramsey. On Sundays there were two trains to Port Erin and two to Peel but none to Ramsey.

In stark contrast the weekday timetable for summer 1963 consisted of four trains from Douglas to Port Erin, two to Peel and two to Ramsey, and a mid-morning service from Ramsey to Kirk Michael and back. Buses were provided for the advertised late afternoon services to both Peel and Ramsey. The only trains on Sundays were those to Kirk Braddan in connection with the regular open-air church services.

In 1967, under Lord Ailsa, trains ran from 3rd June until the end of September. On Mondays to Saturdays, during the peak tourist season, nine were scheduled to leave the capital bound for Peel, a further three for Ramsey, and four to Castletown. On Sundays six travelled the line to Peel, one to Ramsey and three to Castletown.

In respect of the northern routes, the 1967 timetable proved much too ambitious. Thus in 1968 Ailsa reduced the peak weekday service between Douglas and Peel to four trains with two to Ramsey on Mondays, Wednesdays and Fridays only, along with a fill in turn from Ramsey to Kirk Michael and return. As the previous year, four trains served the 'south line' and with the track reinstated beyond Castletown these continued through to Port Erin. On Sundays there were two trains along both the Peel and Port Erin lines. For the rest of his tenure from 1969 to 1971, Ailsa maintained a Mondays to Fridays four-train summer service on the 'south line' only. No trains ran at weekends.

When the Isle of Man Railway resumed control in 1972, the established pattern of four weekday return services along the 'south line' during the summer season was retained. Eventually seven days a week running became the norm from 1987. Additionally, from 1989, on Mondays to Thursdays during selected weeks of July and August, two extras featured each way, although these were discontinued from 2005. While the timetable is still very much geared to the needs of the tourist, a recent innovation has been the introduction of commuter trains during the period of the TT races to relieve pressure on the roads.

BUS CONNECTIONS FOR STEAM TRAIN				
DERBY CASTLE	9.29	11.19	1.49	3.49
VILLA MARINA	9.33	11.23	1.53	3.53
RAILWAY STN	9.45	11.35	2.05	4.05
TO PORT ERIN	AM	AM	PM	PM
DOUGLAS	10.10	11.45	2.10	4.10
PORT SODERICK	10.23	11.58	2.23	4.23
BALLASALLA	10.45	12.20	2.45	4.45
CASTLETOWN	10.52	12.28	2.52	4.52
COLBY	11.03	12.38	3.03	5.03
PORT ST MARY	11.12	12.47	3.12	5.12
PORT ERIN	11.15	12.50	3.15	5.15
BUS CONNECTIONS FOR MANX ELECTRIC RAILWAY				
RAILWAY STN	11.25	1.15	3.25	5.25
VILLA MARINA	11.34	1.24	3.34	5.34
DERBY CASTLE	11.38	1.28	3.38	5.38

From Douglas: Santon 25 mins; Ballabeg 47 mins; Level 56 mins.
From Port Erin: Level 8 mins, Ballabeg 17 mins; Santon 42 mins.
822275 • Port Erin 833432.

April to October 1993

DOUGLAS - BALLASALLA - CASTLETOWN - PORT ST MARY - PORT ERIN

		A			A					A			A	
DOUGLAS	1000	1035	1200	1400	1435	1615	PORT ERIN	1015	1140	1215	1415	1555	1630
Port Soderick	1012	1047	1212	1412	1447	1627	Port St Mary	1019	1144	1219	1419	1559	1634
Santon	1022	1057	1222	1422	1457	1637	Colby	1027	1152	1227	1427	1607	1642
Ballasalla	1032	1107	1232	1432	1507	1647	Castletown	1038	1203	1238	1438	1618	1653
Castletown	1039	1114	1239	1439	1514	1654	Ballasalla	1045	1210	1245	1445	1625	1700
Colby	1049	1124	1249	1449	1524	1704	Santon	1056	1221	1256	1456	1636	1711
Port St Mary	1057	1132	1257	1457	1532	1712	Port Soderick	1105	1230	1305	1505	1645	1720
PORT ERIN	1100	1135	1300	1500	1535	1715	DOUGLAS	1117	1242	1317	1517	1657	1732

A - Runs Monday to Thursday 17 July to 24 August ONLY

BY REQUEST train stops at Santon, Ronaldsway, Ballabeg and Level. TO ALIGHT inform guard on boarding. TO BOARD give clear hand signal to the driver.

April to October 2000

Douglas - Santon - Ballasalla - Castletown

Douglas	10.00	12.00	14.15	16.15
Pt Soderick	10.12	12.12	14.27	16.27
Santon	10.21	12.21	14.36	16.36
Ballasalla	10.30	12.30	14.45	16.45
Castletown	10.36	12.36	14.51	16.51

April to May 2004

Douglas - Santon - Ballasalla - Castletown - Port St Mary - Port Erin

Douglas	10.10	11.50	13.50	15.20	16.40
Pt Soderick	10.22	12.02	14.02	15.32	16.52
Santon	10.31	12.11	14.11	15.41	17.01
Ballasalla	10.40	12.20	14.20	15.50	17.10
Castletown	10.47	12.27	14.27	15.57	17.17
Ballabeg	10.52	12.32	14.32	16.02	17.22
Colby	10.57	12.37	14.37	16.07	17.27
Port St. Mary	11.04	12.44	14.44	16.14	17.34
Port Erin	11.07	12.47	14.47	16.17	17.37

May to October 2004

Departs

					TT Trains
Douglas	10.20	12.20	14.20	16.20	17.45
Pt Soderick	10.32	12.32	14.32	16.32	17.57
Santon	10.41	12.41	14.41	16.41	18.06
Ballasalla	10.50	12.50	14.50	16.50	18.15
Castletown	10.57	12.57	14.57	16.57	18.22
Colby	11.07	13.07	15.07	17.07	18.32
Port St. Mary	11.14	13.14	15.14	17.14	18.39
Port Erin	11.17	13.17	15.17	17.17	18.42

Daily from Monday 6th April to Sunday 27th September 2009

TT Trains - Only run from Monday 1st June to Friday 5th June and Monday 8th June to Thursday 11th June 2009

April to September 2009

Douglas	10.20	14.20		Port Erin	12.20	16.20
Pt Soderick	10.32	14.32		Port St. Mary	12.24	16.24
Santon	10.41	14.41		Colby	12.31	16.31
Ballasalla	10.50	14.50		Castletown	12.42	16.42
Castletown	10.57	14.57		Ballasalla	12.50	16.50
Colby	11.07	15.07		Santon	12.58	16.58
Port St. Mary	11.14	15.14		Pt Soderick	13.06	17.06
Port Erin	11.17	15.17		Douglas	13.17	17.17

Trains stop BY REQUEST at Santon, Ronaldsway Halt, Ballabeg and Colby Level.
TO ALIGHT inform the Guard on boarding.
TO BOARD give a clear hand signal to the Driver.

September to November 2009

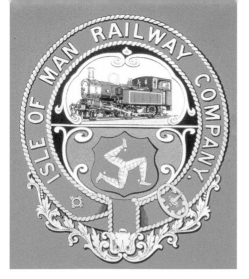

1. The current Isle of Man Railway Company crest as carried on the cab side sheets of the Beyer Peacock 2-4-0Ts. It includes the ancient symbol of the island, the Three Legs of Man, and a portrait of no.16 *Mannin*, identifiable by the square-shaped cab. An earlier version featured a side profile of one of the smaller 2-4-0Ts with a bell-mouthed dome and Salter safety valves. (T.Heavyside)

LOCOMOTIVES

Remarkably, at the start of the 1960s all but four of the steam locomotives owned from 1873 by the Isle of Man and Manx Northern railways were still extant. The casualties were two Sharp Stewart 2-4-0Ts bought by the MNR in 1879, and two IoMR 2-4-0Ts nos 2 *Derby* and 7 *Tynwald*.

Down the years the IoMR has relied mainly on a fleet of 2-4-0T locomotives manufactured by Beyer Peacock & Co Ltd of Gorton Foundry, Manchester. The initial batch of three were shipped to the island during spring 1873 equipped with 11in diameter and 18in stroke outside cylinders, and 3ft 9in diameter wheels. The side tanks held 320 gallons of water.

IoMR nos 4 to 9 arrived on the island between 1874 and 1896, as did MNR no.3 (later IoMR no.14) *Thornhill* in 1880. These seven were built to the same drawings as the earlier 2-4-0Ts supplied by Beyer Peacock except they had larger side tanks able to hold 385 gallons, nos 1 to 3 being similarly modified later.

Meanwhile the Manx Northern had also purchased an 0-6-0T, no.4 (later IoMR no.15) *Caledonia* from Dübs & Co of Glasgow in 1885. Fitted with 13½in x 20in outside cylinders and 3ft 3in diameter wheels, at 85% of maximum boiler pressure of 140lbs per square inch tractive effort was 11,120lbs, making it the most powerful engine ever to work on the island. It was also the heaviest, turning the scales at 23 tons 11cwt in full working order.

During the years 1905 to 1910 the IoMR imported a further four 2-4-0Ts from Beyer Peacock, nos 10 to 13. These had slightly larger 3ft 3in diameter boilers and 480 gallon tanks, and stood 5in taller than the earlier examples at 9ft 11in above rail level.

The last locomotive ordered from Beyer Peacock, no.16 *Mannin*, left their factory in 1926. It was the largest and most powerful of the 2-4-0Ts. The main differences compared to the older engines were 12in diameter cylinders, a 3ft 6in diameter boiler able to withstand a maximum pressure of 180lbs per square inch, providing a nominal tractive effort of 8,810lbs. The tanks held 520 gallons of water, the bunker 1½ tons of coal, and in full working order weighed 23 tons 9cwt. Its bulkier profile and square-shaped cab gave it a distinctive appearance.

Various detail modifications have been made to the locomotives over the years, the most significant being replacement 3ft 3in diameter boilers fitted to nos 1 to 8 which increased their maximum height to 9ft 11in as per nos 10 to 13.

The standard livery during the early 1960s, as introduced in 1945, was Indian red with yellow and black lining. In 1967 Lord Ailsa changed this to apple green with black and white lining. Since 1980 the working engines have sported a variety of colours.

As regards diesel power, two Walker Bros of Wigan railcars, nos 19 and 20, were obtained in 1961 from the closed County Donegal Railways Joint Committee in Ireland. Many years later, two small four-wheeled diesel-mechanical locomotives, built at the Motor Rail Ltd, Simplex Works, Bedford, were obtained second-hand for shunting and light duties, the first in 1987 and the second in 1996. In the interim, in 1992, the railway took delivery from Germany of a four-wheeled diesel-hydraulic locomotive built in 1958, no.17 *Viking*, for works trains and emergency use.

    A further two diesel locomotives have been acquired in recent years. First in 2004 the railway took over a Hunslet-Barclay four-wheeled diesel-hydraulic locomotive that had been brought to the island by contractors relaying the 'south line'. It is now numbered 18 and named *Ailsa*. Then in December 2013 a powerful diesel-electric supplied by Motive Power & Equipment Solutions of Greenville, South Carolina, was imported from the USA for main line use.

    Today, as well as the diesel railcars and locomotives, 12 of the original steam locomotives can be seen either on the railway or in the Port Erin Railway Museum. For completeness the accompanying table gives the present whereabouts or disposal details of all the locomotives that have worked over the Isle of Man Railway.

No.	Builder & Works No.	Year	Name	Location/Disposal
1	BP1253	1873	*Sutherland*	IoMR
1(a)	SS2885	1879	*Ramsey*	Scrapped 1923
2	BP1254	1873	*Derby*	Dismantled 1951
2(a)	SS2886	1879	*Northern*	Scrapped 1912
3	BP1255	1873	*Pender*	Sectioned exhibit Museum of Science & Industry, Manchester
4	BP1416	1874	*Loch*	IoMR
5	BP1417	1874	*Mona*	IoMR
6	BP1524	1875	*Peveril*	Port Erin Railway Museum
7	BP2038	1880	*Tynwald*	Dismantled 1945 – frames etc now at Fengate Farm, Weeting, Norfolk
8	BP3610	1894	*Fenella*	IoMR
9	BP3815	1896	*Douglas*	IoMR
10	BP4662	1905	*G.H.Wood*	IoMR
11	BP4663	1905	*Maitland*	IoMR
12	BP5126	1908	*Hutchinson*	IoMR
13	BP5382	1910	*Kissack*	IoMR
14(a)	BP2028	1880	*Thornhill*	Privately preserved, near Ramsey
15(a)	D2178	1885	*Caledonia*	IoMR
16	BP6296	1926	*Mannin*	Port Erin Railway Museum
17(b)	Sc2086	1958	*Viking*	IoMR
18	HAB770	1990	*Ailsa*	IoMR
19(c)	WkB	1950		IoMR
20(c)	WkB	1951		IoMR
(d)	MR22021	1959		IoMR
(e)	MR40s280	1966		IoMR
21	MPES	2013		IoMR

Notes:
(a) Originally owned by Manx Northern Railway – to IoMR 1905.
(b) ex-Dortmund, Germany 1992.
(c) ex-County Donegal Railways Joint Committee, Ireland 1961.
(d) ex-Miller Engineering & Construction Ltd, Sandiacre, Derbyshire 1987.
(e) ex-Neil Clayton, Ripon, North Yorkshire 1996, previously National Coal Board.

Builders:
BP   Beyer Peacock & Co Ltd, Gorton Foundry, Manchester.
D   Dübs & Co, Glasgow Locomotive Works, Glasgow.
HAB   Hunslet-Barclay Ltd, Caledonia Works, Kilmarnock.
MPES Motive Power & Equipment Solutions, Greenville, South Carolina.
MR   Motor Rail Ltd, Simplex Works, Bedford.
Sc   Christoph Schöttler Maschinenfabrik GmbH, Diepholz, Germany.
SS   Sharp Stewart & Co Ltd, Atlas Works, Manchester.
WkB   Walker Bros (Wigan) Ltd, Pagefield Ironworks, Wigan.

1. Douglas to Peel

DOUGLAS

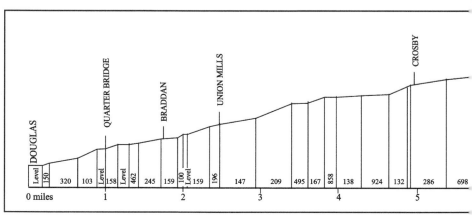

Level		150	320	103	Level	158	Level	462	245	159	100 Level	159	196	147	209	495	167	858	138	924	132	286	698

0 miles   1   2   3   4   5

2. A platform end view looks towards the engine shed and workshops in the summer of 1963. Basking in the sunshine are nos 11 *Maitland* and 12 *Hutchinson*, along with ex-County Donegal railcars nos 19 and 20. The steam engines were both named after directors of the IoMR, William A.Hutchinson serving from 1898 until his death in 1909, while Dalrymple Maitland did likewise from 1899 until his death in 1919. The lower quadrant signals guarded the exits from platforms 1 to 4, which were used by the Peel and Ramsey services. The coaling stage and water column were conveniently placed by the engine release road between platforms 4 and 5. This was especially useful when the timetable demanded a quick turn around and there was little time to visit the shed. (D.Penney)

II. Gradient Profile Douglas to Peel.

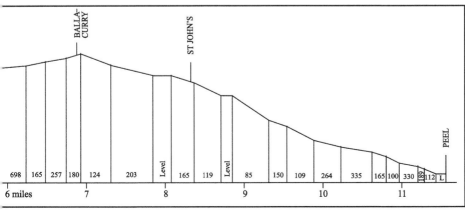

3. The canopies covered most of the length of the platforms. They had protected passengers from the elements since 1909. Here on a rather dull 31st July 1964 the largest and most powerful of the Beyer Peacock 2-4-0Ts no.16 *Mannin* is ready to depart from platforms 3 and 4 with a combined Peel and Ramsey service. A second coal and watering facility can be seen on the right, enabling two locomotives to be serviced simultaneously. The island platform on the right was used by Port Erin line services. (D.J.Mitchell)

4. The driver of the only 0-6-0T on the IoMR no.15 *Caledonia*, at the head of an Isle of Man Railway Supporters Association special to St John's, oils around his charge while waiting in platforms 1 and 2 on a rainy 2nd June 1968. At this time the engine was identified by its former Manx Northern Railway no.4. The leading carriage is 'pairs' no.F75. It was formed in 1926 when the bodies were removed from two four-wheel coaches nos A12 and C9 manufactured in 1873/74 by the Birmingham-based Metropolitan Railway Carriage & Wagon Co, and mounted on a new bogie underframe supplied by the same company. (D.J.Mitchell)

III. Track Plan of Douglas during the 1960s.

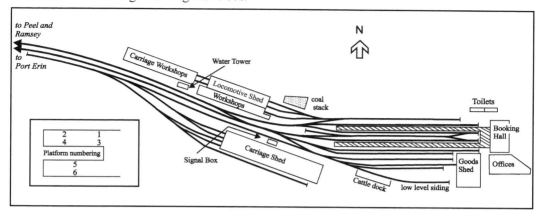

Isle of Man Railway Company
DOUGLAS STATION
(End of Athol Street and Top of Harbour)

GRAND

DAY EXCURSIONS

		Return Fare
PORT ERIN	Travel by 10-20 train. See also the adjacent beauty spot Port St Mary	**4/3**
CASTLETOWN	Travel by 10-20 train. See the former capital & its famous Castle Rushen	**2/9**
PEEL	Travel by 10-25 train. See the Historic Castle and Old-World City	**3/3**
GLEN WYLLIN	Travel by 10-25 train. Spend a day at this delightful Glen.	**4/–**

Motor-Boating Lake, Sandy Shore, Games, Children's Playground. Luncheons, Teas, Snacks at reasonable charges. (SPECIAL FARE, including Luncheon, 8/-)

RAMSEY	Travel by 10-25 train. Visit the Mooragh Park and Swimming Pool (North Promenade)	**4/9**

RUNABOUT TICKET
☞ ONE **10/-** WEEK ☜

BRADDAN

5.   From 1856 open-air church services were held annually in the grounds of Kirk Braddan parish church on Sundays during the summer months. The station was opened in 1897 to cater for the large numbers who attended, being just a short walk from the church; it was only available on Sunday mornings. Return times tended to be flexible, enabling worshippers to join in the final hymn without worrying if they might miss the last train, especially after a long sermon! Here railcars nos 19 and 20 await a full complement of passengers before travelling back to Douglas on Sunday 2nd August 1964. Patiently waiting behind is no.12 *Hutchinson*, which will follow later with a second train. The wooden ticket office remained in place after the line's closure until 1988 when it was dismantled and transported to Colby (see picture 102). The same year the trackbed was designated as a public footpath, and as part of what is now known as the Steam Heritage Trail walkers are able to continue through to Peel. The section of the trail between Quarter Bridge and Braddan is also used as a TT (Tourist Trophy) access road when racing is in progress on the parallel A1 road, times when otherwise residents living within the course would have no means of reaching their properties. (D.J.Mitchell)

UNION MILLS

6.   The platform on the right was laid along with the down loop in 1906/7, but trains ceased to call after 1955. Here nos 11 *Maitland* and 5 *Mona* hurry past with a train from Douglas in May 1963. The brake composite coach immediately behind *Mona*, no.F22, was built by MRCW in 1896. It could seat 42 passengers. Sadly it was one of those destroyed by fire at St John's in 1975 (see picture 15). (D.Penney)

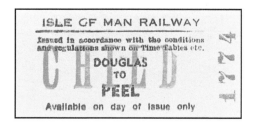

ISLE OF MAN RAILWAY

Issued in accordance with the conditions
and regulations shown on Time Tables etc.

DOUGLAS
TO
PEEL

Available on day of issue only

7.   The next year no.12 *Hutchinson* was photographed at the west end of the station while running round the empty stock of a Douglas to Braddan excursion on Sunday 2nd August 1964 (see picture 5). On the right the redundant ticket office and waiting shelter stand forlorn. The bridge in the background carries the A1 Douglas to Peel road. The station enjoyed a new lease of life from 1967 when reinstated to the timetable by Lord Ailsa. (D.J.Mitchell)

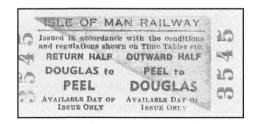

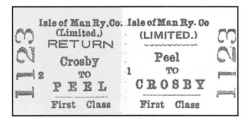

8.   Today the platform remains in situ, along with a short length of track supporting an eight-ton hand crane constructed by Richard C.Gibbins & Co of Birmingham in 1893. Before being positioned here in 1990, the crane had formed part of the breakdown train. It was observed in May 2015 between numerous joggers and walkers enjoying the Steam Heritage Trail. (T.Heavyside)

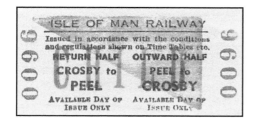

CROSBY

9.   The timber clad building with a brick gable support for the chimney is observed from the rear brake coach of a departing Douglas to Ramsey service on 23rd May 1964. The guard's ducket window is prominent. Behind the train, a member of the station staff attends to the level crossing gates that were swung back and forth across the B35 Crosby to St Mark's road. Up until 1960, a small corrugated iron goods shed had stood by the siding on the left. (R.R.Darsley)

10.   Four years later a 2-4-0T calls with a two-coach westbound service on 2nd June 1968. Little had changed during the intervening period. Just visible beyond the trees on the right is the former crossing-keepers lodge. This is now available as a shelter for those walking the Steam Heritage Trail. All other traces of the former railway were removed in 1976. (D.J.Mitchell)

ST JOHN'S

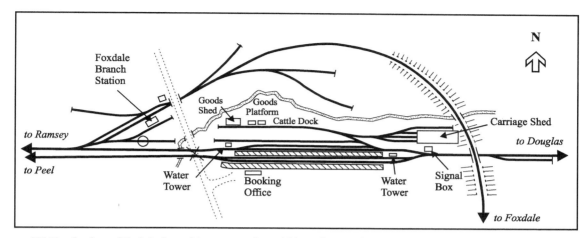

IV. Track plan of St John's and its approaches. Although no trains ran along the Foxdale branch after January 1960, most of the rails remained in situ. Peel trains used the two lines on the south side, those serving Ramsey running along the north side of the layout.

11. No.16 *Mannin* (an ancient name of the island) cautiously enters the south side of the complex with two coaches destined for Peel on 31st July 1964. No.16 had brought a combined Peel and Ramsey service from Douglas and in accordance with normal operating practice had stopped short of the junction points while the Ramsey portion was detached. The driver of no.5 *Mona* (an old Roman name for the island) is about to hand-over the token for the single line section to Peel, before reversing up to the Ramsey train and proceeding along the north side of the station. Note *Mona* has a cast number plate attached to the side tank above the nameplate in addition to the large numeral on the chimney. The wooden signal box supported on a stone base controlled only the eastern end of the site. It housed a ten-lever frame supplied by Stevens & Son of London and Glasgow; there was one spare lever. Behind the box is the 1905-erected, three-road, 288ft-long corrugated iron carriage shed. (D.J.Mitchell)

12.   On a day of intermittent showers, no.16 *Mannin* passes the station building with a train from Peel on 5th August 1964. This proved to be *Mannin's* last year in service, being withdrawn the next month after logging 516,197 miles since arriving on the island in March 1926. The roof of the Central Hotel (now demolished) can be observed behind *Mannin*. (D.J.Mitchell)

13.   A panorama looking in an easterly direction from the island platform in May 1965. The nearest of the three coaches lined up outside the carriage shed is 60-seater third 'pairs' no.F51. This was put together in 1912 when the former bodies from carriages nos B3 and B5, constructed in 1873/74 by MRCW, were placed on a new underframe ordered from the same company. No.F58 behind was similarly formed in 1922 by reusing the bodies from nos B18 and C3. In total 26 such 'pairs' were created between 1909 and 1926, most of the old four-wheeled chassis being adapted as freight wagons. Above the coaches is the inclined embankment whereby Foxdale branch trains gained sufficient height to cross over the Douglas line by the stone bridge visible beyond the signal box. The semaphore signal governing movements from the Ramsey line towards the capital is in the lowered 'off' position, while the corresponding arm of the Peel line signal, to be sighted above the water tower, remains firmly in the horizontal 'stop' position. (D.J.Mitchell)

14. This westward view from July 1967 illustrates the spacious nature of the station. No.11 *Maitland* has just returned from Ramsey with four saloon coaches. The level crossing gates are by the St John's to Castletown road. (D.J.Mitchell)

15. Overlooked by the slopes of the 1383ft-high Greeba Mountain, no.12 *Hutchinson* shunts a couple of coaches outside the carriage shed in August 1968. Like *Mona* (see picture 11) *Hutchinson* has a cast number plate attached to the side tank just above the nameplate, but no number on the chimney. Originally all IoMR locomotives could be identified by polished brass numerals fastened each side of the chimney, but over the years with the exchange and renewal of chimneys these were sometimes dispensed with. Behind the bunker is carriage no.F18, a 50-seater brake composite imported by the IoMR from Brown Marshalls & Co of Birmingham in 1894. After cessation of passenger services on the northern routes in 1968, the carriage shed continued to provide winter storage facilities for stock used on the Port Erin line until 1971. After this a number of redundant carriages were left inside the shed, but on 10th December 1975 a catastrophic fire rendered some almost unidentifiable. The area was cleared in 1976, St John's Primary School now occupying part of the site. (D.Penney)

PEEL

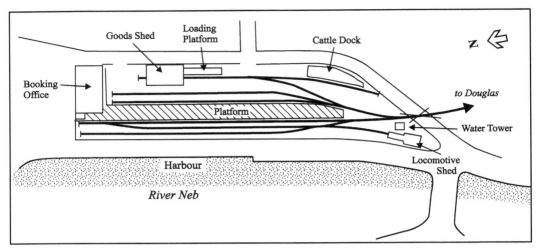

V. Diagram of the layout and buildings at Peel during its latter years.

16. No.12 *Hutchinson* waits 'right away' with an evening excursion back to Douglas in June 1963. Brake third no.F41, constructed by MRCW in 1907, leads the six coach formation. The large goods shed, rising above *Hutchinson*, dated from 1911. Prominent to the left of the station building, behind the Railway Hotel, the tower of St Peter's church points skyward, although since 1958 only the tower and west wall have remained standing. (D.Penney)

17.   During the Whitsuntide Bank Holiday in 1965, no.5 *Mona* is about to run into the station. Note there is no cast number plate on the right-hand side tank as on the opposite side (see picture 11). At the end of the previous year the engine had ran no less than 1,896,370 miles, a further 5,689 being added during 1965. The enginemen's mess hut, and the one-road engine shed on the right, both look in a sorry state. The premises directly behind *Mona*, on the other side of Mill Road, were occupied by T.Moore & Sons Ltd, escallop processors and kipper curers, other renowned Isle of Man delicacies. (D.J.Mitchell)

18.   In June 1968, *Hutchinson*, now in green livery, was photographed again, this time with only three coaches on the harbour side of the island platform. (D.J.Mitchell)

19. No.1 *Sutherland* returned to its old haunts (albeit on a low loader) on Saturday 22nd August 1998 as part of the celebrations to mark the 125th anniversary of the IoMR. With temporary track laid across the old station site, visitors were able to enjoy short footplate rides. Anchored in the harbour at low tide are three replica Viking boats, a vivid reminder of some much earlier visitors to Peel. (T.Heavyside)

Other views of the route to the west coast of the island can be seen in our *Douglas to Peel* album.

'Steam 125' postage stamps celebrating 125 years of Isle of Man Railways (1873-1998).

20. On the same day a panoramic view of the town and harbour was obtained from the slopes of the headland. The former station building, just in front of *Sutherland*, has been incorporated into the House of Manannan, an interactive museum, one of a number of attractions across the island detailing 'The Story of Mann'. Until 1968 it was possible from this standpoint to follow for a short distance the progress of trains heading up the coastline north of St Germain's, as they made their way towards Ramsey. (T.Heavyside)

21. The large water tank, held aloft by an equally substantial stone tower, by the former Mill Road level crossing, forms the centrepiece of a display created by Peel Heritage Trust. As the sign by the base explains, it 'commemorates the first passenger railway on the island, Douglas to Peel 11½ miles 1873-1968'. The exhibits include a level crossing gate straddling a short length of track, a signal windlass by the foot of the left-hand post, and a lower quadrant signal from Lezayre. Behind the neat platform is the body of coach no.C1, built by MRCW in 1873. In 1912 it was paired with the body from another four-wheeler no.B19 of the same vintage on a new bogie underframe, both from the same source, to form 60-seater third class vehicle no.F64. This evocative scene was photographed on 10th September 2006. Just across the road, behind the cameraman, the old brickworks office has been converted into a transport museum, where further items of railway interest can be studied. (T.Heavyside)

2. St John's to Foxdale

VI. Gradient profile for St John's to Foxdale.

ST JOHN'S

22. The former Foxdale Railway premises, complete with decorative yellow quoins, was erected in 1886. After the FR was taken over by the IoMR in 1905 the building was converted to a dwelling house for the station master. Branch trains ceased to call here from 1927, instead reversing in and out of the main station. This was the scene looking towards Foxdale in May 1965, the former platform having become submerged under some lush vegetation, as had any rails that might remain. The structure on the left once supported a water tank, while above the station, on the opposite side of the road, can be seen the Railway Junction Hotel. The latter is now used as offices. (D.J.Mitchell)

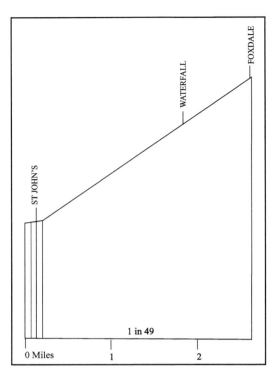

ST JOHN'S

WATERFALL

FOXDALE

1 in 49

0 Miles   1   2

WATERFALL

23. This was the only intermediate stopping place on the branch. It served the village of Lower Foxdale but took its name from the nearby Hamilton Waterfall. It is a peaceful spot as evidenced by this view looking in the direction of St John's in May 1960, and while the rails remained securely in position the wooden hut that adorned the site from circa 1905 had disappeared. In the background Slieau Whallian rises to 1094ft above sea level. Today the trackbed is used as a footpath. (D.J.Mitchell)

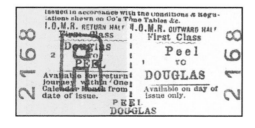

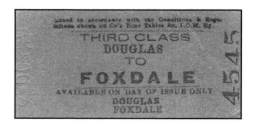

FOXDALE

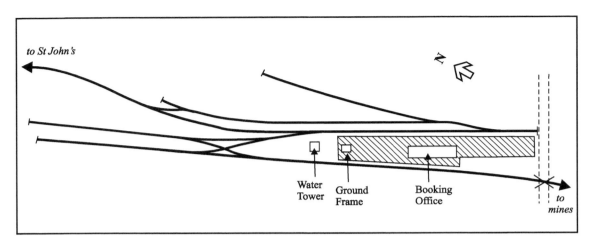

VII. Track plan of the Foxdale station area. Some track materials were recovered in January 1960, although most of the layout remained in position until the mid-1970s.

24.   For many years the area was blighted by vast heaps of waste material from quarrying activities, as witnessed when the photographer visited on 4th August 1964. The yellow quoins incorporated into the red brick station building stand out. The water tower supporting a cylindrical tank was of similar construction. The buildings in the middle distance were owned by a local quarrying company, which for a time had use of the station premises. Trains needing access to the mining complex had first to reverse by the station platform, then again in the sidings on the right, before proceeding cautiously up the steep incline behind the station and across the A24 road from Douglas on the level. In the distance are the lower slopes of South Barrule, which at its peak, some two miles south-west of this point, reaches an altitude of 1586ft above sea level. (D.J.Mitchell)

25. Although over 50 years have passed since any steam locomotive ventured down the branch, the station building still stands. After being relinquished by the quarrying company it was later utilised for various community purposes; it is currently the home of Foxdale Heritage. In this scene from May 2015 the path following the old line lies straight ahead, while on the right the grounds of the 1991-built Foxdale Primary School extend across former railway land. (T.Heavyside)

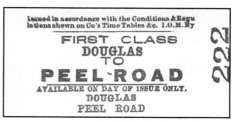

3. St John's to Ramsey

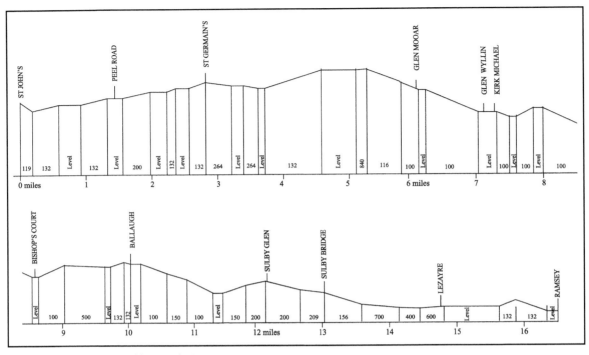

VIII. Gradient profile St John's to Ramsey.

WEST OF ST JOHN'S

26.   For almost half-a-mile the Ramsey and Peel lines ran side by side, before parting company after passing over the River Neb by means of independent 30ft-long wrought iron bridges. Trains for the two destinations often departed St John's simultaneously, and leading on this occasion in July 1959, about to diverge north towards Peel Road, is a Ramsey bound service with no.6 *Peveril* in charge. Trailing behind, just crossing the Neb, a sister 2-4-0T heads for Peel. (C.Hogg/Colour-Rail.com)

ST GERMAIN'S

27. For four years until Peel Road opened in 1883, this was the nearest Manx Northern Railway station to Peel, albeit a two-mile trek from the centre of the town. It officially closed in July 1961. The fine red sandstone building, inhabited as a house from 1906, is shown to good effect as no.10 *G.H.Wood* approaches with a lightly loaded two-coach train from Ramsey in June 1968. Both the corrugated iron shed on the right and the trackbed look somewhat neglected. (D.J.Mitchell)

28. Nowadays it is hikers rather than Beyer Peacock 2-4-0Ts that tread the 3½-mile stretch from here to Glen Mooar. The former trackbed also forms part of the 95-mile long Raad ny Foillan (Road of the Gull) circular footpath around the Manx coast. A sign to the right of the kissing gate outlines the path's railway ancestry. Various improvements have been made to the property (now privately owned) in recent times, including new windows on the first floor of the two gables, while an extension on the south side has replaced the old shed. The scene was recorded looking towards St John's on 18th May 2002. (T.Heavyside)

29. In sight of the Irish Sea, no.5 *Mona* was observed to the north of the headland at Gob-y-Deigan as it hastened towards Ramsey in May 1963. The passengers were no doubt enjoying the spectacular nature of the surrounds. In the distance, St Patrick's Isle, guarding the entrance to Peel Harbour, can be discerned, as can the 50ft-high tower on Corrins Hill that rises 485ft above the town. (D.Penney)

GLEN MOOAR

30. While looking out to sea no.12 *Hutchinson* rides high 75ft above the floor of the river as it crosses the 180ft-long viaduct and heads towards Ramsey in June 1963. The three lattice steel girders of equal length replaced the original wrought iron structure in 1921. Today only the masonry pillars and buttresses survive, the girders having been dismantled in 1975. The glen itself is now designated a Manx National Glen, one of seventeen on the island, and it is still possible to follow the path leading inland on the left to reach the site of Spooyt Vane (White Spout) waterfall, one of the highest on the island. (D.Penney)

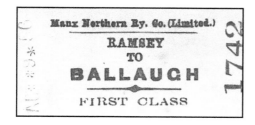

Manx Northern Ry. Co. (Limited.)
RAMSEY
TO
BALLAUGH
FIRST CLASS
1742

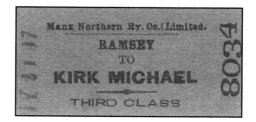

Manx Northern Ry. Co. (Limited.
RAMSEY
TO
KIRK MICHAEL
THIRD CLASS
8034

GLEN WYLLIN

31. When the viaduct was first built three 65ft-long iron lattice girders supported the rails across the glen, but were superseded by plate girders in 1915. Here no.11 *Maitland* slows on the approach to Kirk Michael in July 1967. This was a special working consisting of four open vestibule coaches manufactured by MRCW in 1905. That next to the engine is no.F31. As regards the 20-acre glen, this was developed as a tourist attraction from the 1890s and became very popular with day excursionists. In 1935 the IoMR acquired the grounds and developed the facilities further, with patrons being able to partake in activities such as boating, bowls, dancing and tennis, as well as enjoying concerts or a quiet stroll down to the shore. The glen's popularity declined in later years and it was subsequently sold into private hands. (D.J.Mitchell)

32. In 1975, in common with the viaduct at Glen Mooar, the girders were dismantled and scrapped, the buttresses and pillars being left standing. Three years later the glen became Government property and subsequently given status as a Manx National Glen. In the background to this panorama, looking inland on 18th May 2002, is the rounded summit of Slieau Freoaghane at 1601ft above sea level. (T.Heavyside)

KIRK MICHAEL

33. This was a busy station in the days when Glen Wyllin was popular, a convenient footpath along the eastern side of the line providing an easy access route to the glen. Here the railcars bide time by the red sandstone, slate-roofed station building on a damp day in June 1967. The railcars are wearing a slightly revised paint scheme compared to earlier years (see picture 5). With no turntables available the units were always operated coupled back-to-back. Significantly, after their acquisition in 1961 they were used extensively, for instance in 1964 they covered a distance of 13,809 miles, more than 30% of the total engine mileage that year and over double that of any steam locomotive. The goods shed, constructed in 1923, is on the left. Beyond the level crossing gates is the water tank positioned near the end of the single line section from St Germain's, where it could be used by steam locomotives travelling in either direction. (D.J.Mitchell)

34. After closure, the Isle of Man Fire Service took over the buildings, with the goods shed being adapted to house the fire engine. A redundant level crossing gate and a short length of track remind passers by of its earlier life. In May 2002 part of the highway had worn away to reveal a short section of rails embedded in the surface. (T.Heavyside)

BALLAUGH

35.   An unhindered view of the station buildings and goods shed looking towards St John's on 1st August 1964. The points connecting the siding leading to the goods shed and the goods loop were behind the photographer. The remains of the goods platform can be discerned on the right. The level crossing gates protected vehicles travelling along the A10 road that follows a circuitous route from Ballaugh around the north of the island via Jurby and Bride to Ramsey. (D.J.Mitchell)

36.   Four years later and the trackbed appears somewhat overgrown as no.10 *G.H.Wood* calls with a Douglas to Ramsey service on 3rd June 1968. Named after George Henry Wood, the first company secretary of the IoMR who continued in office until 1903, the locomotive had by this time clocked over one million miles. Since 1979, when the area was smartened up as a Manx Millennium project, it has been known as Ballaugh Park. In 1995 the local cubs were responsible for renovating the goods shed, while in 2014 it was opened as a visitor centre by Ballaugh Heritage Trust with displays featuring the village as well as the railway. A modern bungalow has replaced the old station premises. (D.J.Mitchell)

WILD LIFE PARK

37. No.11 *Maitland* prepares to halt with a train from Douglas in July 1967. This only became a calling place in 1965, the same year the Curraghs Wildlife Park was opened on the adjacent wetlands by the IoM Government. During its first season it was known as Ballavolley Halt for Wild Life Park, but under Lord Ailsa became plain Wild Life Park. The park's perimeter fence is on the right, the entrance being adjacent to the level crossing by the gatekeepers-lodge (now privately owned) in the left background. Today the park remains a popular attraction, a diverse range of animals and birds, originating from many corners of the world, being housed in conditions resembling that of their homelands. While regrettably it is no longer possible to travel to the park by rail, there is still a railway presence within the grounds in the form of a quite splendid miniature railway. Known as 'The Orchid Line' it is operated by the Manx Steam & Model Engineering Club. Locomotives of three different gauges can often be seen in action, some travelling a half-mile circuit of 5in and 7¼in dual gauge track, while a shorter 600ft length accommodates engines with wheels set to a width of 3½in. (D.J.Mitchell)

SULBY GLEN

38.   Five intending passengers greet the arrival of no.8 *Fenella* on its way to Ramsey on 1st August 1964. The raised platform and building date from 1910. The level crossing gates are astride the A14 road that threads the highly scenic Sulby Glen, from which the station took its name. The road ends high in the Northern Upland Massif at the Bungalow, the only intermediate station on the Snaefell Mountain Railway (see pictures 73 to 76 in our *Douglas-Laxey-Ramsey* album). Following closure of the railway, the station building was redesigned as a private dwelling, extra living space being provided by a new outer wall close to the edge of the old platform, leaving only two of the decorated stanchions exposed, these now effectively supporting a veranda over the front door. (D.J.Mitchell)

39.   The cameraman stood on the disused goods platform to record no.11 *Maitland* leaving in the opposite direction in July 1967. The one siding is partially visible on the right. The trackbed of the main line has since been fenced off as a footpath, while the rest of the area in view provides a pleasant garden for the present occupants of the premises. (D.J.Mitchell)

SULBY BRIDGE

40.   No.10 *G.H.Wood* hurries away with two coaches forming a Ramsey to Douglas service on 3rd June 1968. Behind the train the crossing-keeper steps purposely towards the level crossing gates to reopen them to traffic using the A17 Sulby to Bride road. The course of the lifted goods siding, that also served the cattle dock, is evident on the right. The former Manx Northern Railway station building is hidden from sight by the foliage to the right of the running lines. It was sold into private hands during the mid-1970s, with the modernised and extended structure now appropriately named Railway House. (D.J.Mitchell)

LEZAYRE

41. Situated in a pleasant location between the A3 and A13 roads leading out of Ramsey, it was sometimes referred to as Garey, the name of the nearby village. From 1908 it became a 'request stop', and while omitted from the timetables altogether from September 1950, trains continued to stop as and when required. It was reinstated to the timetable under Lord Ailsa in 1967. After the line's closure the stone station building stood forlorn and neglected for many years but was put back in good order and converted to a private residence during the 1990s. Yellow brick quoins highlight the corners, door and window surrounds. This westward view, from where the level crossing gates once stood was recorded in April 2001. Sadly the rails no longer extend much beyond the edge of the property. (T.Heavyside)

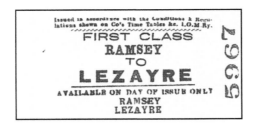

Issued in accordance with the Conditions & Regulations shewn on Co's Time Tables &c. I.O.M.Ry.

FIRST CLASS

RAMSEY
TO
LEZAYRE

AVAILABLE ON DAY OF ISSUE ONLY
RAMSEY
LEZAYRE

RAMSEY

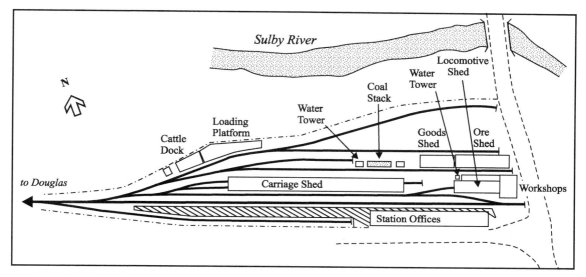

IX. Track Plan of Ramsey during the 1960s. The siding on the north side formerly extended across Bowring Road and along the south side of the harbour. The harbour line was last used in 1949 and any remaining rails lifted in 1957.

42.   On then to the erstwhile headquarters of the Manx Northern Railway and where on 23rd May 1964 little had changed since MNR days. The train on the left had just terminated, while beyond the timber canopy, near the buffer stops, a 2-4-0T is in process of running round the stock. More coaches take up space in the bay platform on the right as an IoMR lorry bides time awaiting its next local deliveries. (R.R.Darsley)

43.   While looking in the opposite direction on a damp 6th August 1964, no.8 *Fenella* travels in reverse gear alongside the two-road carriage shed. The name conferred on the engine was that of a central character in Sir Walter Scott's classic novel *Peveril of the Peak*, first published in 1823. By the end of 1964 *Fenella* had amassed almost 1,348,000 miles. (D.J.Mitchell)

Isle of Man Railways and Tramways postage stamps

44.   On the north side of the layout no.10 *G.H.Wood* shunts a four-wheeled G van in July 1967. The gap in the stone wall is where the track formerly extended across Bowring Road to gain access to the harbour. The tracks either side of the lofty water tower served the goods and ore sheds. (D.J.Mitchell)

45.   Later the same day no.10 stands outside the stone-built one-road engine shed. The nearest section was added in 1886 following purchase of *Caledonia* by the MNR; the demarcation between the original and 'new' sections is evident. Visible to the left is a second water tower along with the south walls of the ore and goods sheds. The buildings were demolished in 1978. (D.J.Mitchell)

46.   The products of Ramsey Bakery are relished throughout the island. Their premises now occupy the site. They were photographed on 25th October 2003 from a similar viewpoint as picture 119 in our *Douglas to Ramsey* album. (T.Heavyside)

Further pictures of the lines between Douglas and Ramsey, and along the Foxfield branch, can be enjoyed in our *Douglas to Ramsey* album.

47.   Although the last of the harbour rails were removed in 1957, it is still possible to envisage the route by walking close to the harbour wall as here in October 2003. The swing bridge, to be seen a little further downstream, was manufactured by the Cleveland Bridge & Engineering Company of Darlington in 1892 and links the north and south banks of the River Sulby. (T.Heavyside)

4. Douglas to Port Erin

DOUGLAS

48.   We now return to the capital, perhaps by way of the still-operative Manx Electric Railway and the Douglas Horse Tramway, and maybe stopping off en route at Laxey to sample the delights of the Snaefell Mountain and Great Laxey Mine railways, and again at Groudle for the Groudle Glen Railway. Journeys along all these railways can be savoured in our *Douglas-Laxey-Ramsey* album. The imposing gateway dating from 1891 (the clock tower was restored in 1990) is seen from the junction of Peel Road and Athol Street on a wet 7th May 1997. Three flights of steps lead down to the station forecourt. The two pedestrians approaching the traffic signals have just walked up Bank Hill from near the harbour. A chimney and part of the station roof is visible on the left. (T.Heavyside)

49. The impressive two-storey, Ruabon brick building, also completed in 1891, is viewed from the road entrance at the bottom of Bank Hill on 9th May 1997. (T.Heavyside)

50. Regrettably, once inside the spacious booking hall, it is no longer possible to purchase tickets to stations along the routes to Peel and Ramsey, although intending passengers in 1997 may have been misled by the board outside the hatch. To avoid confusion the board was later removed to the Port Erin Railway Museum. Pleasingly, a second hatch, out of sight to the left of the board advising 'Book Here Port Erin Line Stations', and once used for first class tickets to all destinations, remains open for business. The large map of the island highlights not only the railway system but also the main omnibus routes, the latter also operated by the IoMR from 1928. The poster on the right directs passengers to the equally delightful Manx Electric and Snaefell Mountain railways. Since 1991 most of the hall has been leased as a cafeteria, extra space being provided by the addition of a mezzanine floor. Numerous railway models, artefacts and memorabilia add to the ambience. The interior was revamped during 2016. (T.Heavyside)

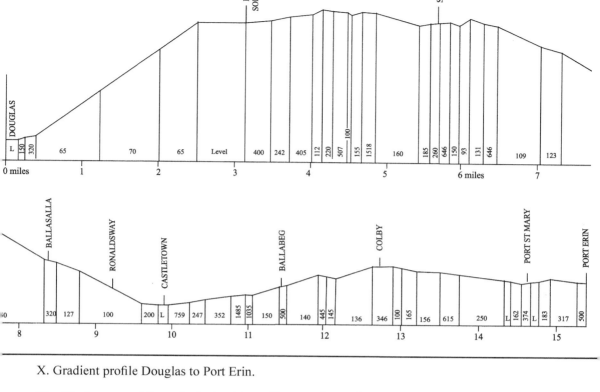

X. Gradient profile Douglas to Port Erin.

51. Having passed through the booking office, an elevated position at the top of the signal box steps enables us to study much of the layout. In the foreground no.13 *Kissack* shunts a rake of stock into platform 6 during June 1973. Nearest the camera is carriage no.F25, a 60-seater brake third, which arrived on the island from the Birmingham-based Metropolitan Railway Carriage & Wagon Works in 1896. Stabled near the buffer stops at the end of platform 3 are five out of service locomotives, while a range of passenger and goods vehicles stand idle in the goods yard on the right. (D.J.Mitchell)

52.   On the same sunny day as the previous picture, a sister 2-4-0T carries out yet more shunting manoeuvres. The signal box on the right, close by the north elevation of the carriage shed, was installed by Dutton & Co Ltd of Worcester, together with the signalling equipment, in 1892. The four-road, 320ft-long corrugated iron carriage shed was erected the following year. The rails nearest the water tower and south wall of the workshops was the preserve of Peel and Ramsey services. The three arms attached to the left-hand post of the bracket signal were lowered as appropriate to allow trains approaching from the west to enter the complex, while the two on the adjacent post controlled trains coming off the Port Erin route. (D.J.Mitchell)

53. Later in June 1973 no.4 *Loch* nears journeys end with a train from Port Erin. The engine took its name from Sir Henry Brougham Loch who was Governor of the island from 1863 until 1882. *Loch* has now accumulated over 1,600,000 miles. (D.Penney)

54. In September of the following year a quintet of locomotives were again on display alongside platform 3. From front to rear they are nos 14 *Thornhill* (originally MNR no.3), 3 *Pender*, 1 *Sutherland*, 16 *Mannin* and 15 *Caledonia*. The three engines nearest the camera all have bell-mouthed domes. No.14 was withdrawn in 1963 after completing 1,478,231 miles since coming into the ownership of the IoMR in April 1905, while no.3 last ran in 1959 with a recorded mileage of 1,247,623. Thornhill was the home of Manx Northern Railway Chairman J.T.Clucas, no.3 perpetuating the name of Sir John Pender, a founding Director and later Chairman of the IoMR. These two locomotives have since left the railway, and while *Thornhill* remains on the island at a private location, *Pender* is now located not far from its birthplace as a sectioned exhibit at the Museum of Science & Industry in Manchester. Ironically there were times during the 1970s, as witnessed here, when the former northern lines platforms were used by a local garage for the storage of new cars and vans. (D.J.Mitchell)

55. During the four years from 1978 the station underwent a radical transformation. First the platform canopies were removed then in 1980 an additional platform was installed along the north side of the layout. In 1982 platforms 5 and 6 were abandoned and along with the old goods yard, given over to car and bus parking. The same year the signal box was decommissioned and the semaphore signals replaced by colour lights activated from the station office, the points then being moved by local levers. Eleven years on and no.12 *Hutchinson* prepares to pilot no.10 *G.H.Wood* away from the rationalised station with the 2.10pm service to Port Erin on 31st August 1993. The next three pictures were taken on the same day. (T.Heavyside)

➡ 56. Locomotives normally work smokebox first out of Douglas, but for a short period in 1993 maroon-liveried no.4 *Loch* ran facing the opposite direction. Here *Loch* takes water from the standpipe located just inside the shed doorway. Note the polished bell-shaped dome. (T.Heavyside)

57. The two ex-County Donegal Railways railcars have not seen regular service since the late 1960s. Here in the shed yard no.19, sporting a faded red and white livery, enjoys a rare glimpse of the sunshine. Renovation work on the railcars started in 1998 but was suspended two years later. (T.Heavyside)

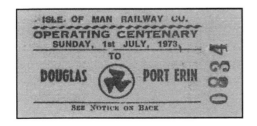

58.   No.12 *Hutchinson*, resplendent in dark blue with a distinctive square-shaped cab and taller side tanks as fitted in 1980, stands on the workshop road with no.17 *Viking*. Note no.12 no longer has a cast number plate on the side tank (see picture 15) but the chimney numerals have been restored. (T.Heavyside)

59.   A number of gala events were held during the 1990s, usually on a grand scale. During one such festive occasion on 18th July 1996, under some strong floodlights rigged up for the evening, no less than five engines were on display. On the left, on what is normally reserved as the engine release road, is no.4 *Loch* with nos 6 *Peveril* and 17 *Viking* behind. On the right nos 15 *Caledonia* and 10 *G.H.Wood* stand with a rake of stock. We can also see part of the platform laid in 1980 alongside the north boundary wall. (T.Heavyside)

60. On the same balmy evening we are able to enjoy a rear three-quarter view of *Peveril*, still sandwiched between *Loch* and *Viking*. Inspiration for the name carried by no.6 came from Sir Walter Scott's novel *Peveril of the Peak*. The engine has not seen service since 1960 at which time it had travelled a staggering 1,924,038 miles. (T.Heavyside)

61. No.11 *Maitland* peeps out from the open doorway at the back of the engine shed, again on 18th July 1996. The locomotive was supplying steam for demonstration purposes to a single-cylinder horizontal engine housed in the adjacent workshops. The engine was built by John Chadwick & Son of Prince's Bridge Ironworks, Manchester, and came second-hand from a cotton mill at Accrington, Lancashire, in 1920. Coupled to an old locomotive boiler it powered the workshop machinery by means of overhead line shafting until 1954. This interesting stationary engine is illustrated in our *Douglas to Port Erin* album (picture 37), while since 2014 visitors to the Port Erin Railway Museum have been able to study it first-hand. The open section, between the back of the engine shed and the carriage workshops, was roofed-over in 1998 to provide additional covered accommodation. (T.Heavyside)

62. Early morning on 7th May 1997 and no.10 *G.H.Wood* has just emerged from the shed into daylight. Partly visible on the right is the body of former Manx Northern Railway first class carriage no.2, one of 14 coaches built by the Swansea Wagon Company for the MNR in 1879. It was renumbered F41 then N41 by the IoMR, serving as the shed mess hut from 1964 until its removal in 1999. It was repositioned here in 2013 for use as an oil store. Douglas Head forms a backdrop with a gasometer prominent below. (T.Heavyside)

63.   Two days later no.17 *Viking* has just returned from a trip to Port Soderick on weed-killing duties. The chemicals and spraying equipment are carried on bogie wagon no.F23. Originally this provided the underframe of a 42-seater brake composite coach constructed by MRCW in 1896. The body was destroyed in 1983. (T.Heavyside)

64.   On the same day this colourful line-up was recorded inside the two-road shed. The engines are nos 12 *Hutchinson*, 9 *Douglas*, 4 *Loch*, 6 *Peveril* and 1 *Sutherland*. (T.Heavyside)

65.   Venturing further into the depths of the shed no.1 *Sutherland* (with its boiler and cab removed) is now nearest the camera. (T.Heavyside)

Isle of Man Railways and Tramways postage stamps

66. The workshops attached to the south wall of the engine shed date from 1891, the rear extension being added in 1906. No.15 *Caledonia* was receiving attention in May 1997. Behind a new boiler awaits fitting to one of the 2-4-0Ts. (T.Heavyside)

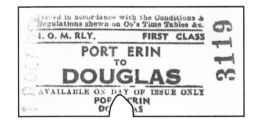

67. On occasions the workshop facilities have been made available to the 2ft 0in gauge Groudle Glen Railway. In May 1997 a privately-built 0-4-2T, similar to a Bagnall engine exported to New Zealand in 1911, was nearing completion. It was later named *Annie*. (T.Heavyside)

68. After many years of inactivity, no.15 *Caledonia* was returned to service in 1995, in time for its centenary celebrations. The 0-6-0T was released from the workshops in its earlier guise as Manx Northern Railway no.4 in a Tuscan red livery and fully lined out. The MNR crest was stencilled on the sandbox with the Dübs diamond-shaped makers plate attached to the cab side sheet. Here in the shed yard the fireman is busy shovelling coal onto the footplate, while the driver oils round the motion in preparation for yet another trip to Port Erin on 22nd August 1998. The tank on the left contains the oil supply for the diesel locomotives. (T.Heavyside)

69.   In 1999 the platform on the north side was lifted and replaced by a siding. While track relaying work was in progress around the station throat, the blue-liveried Motor Rail four-wheeled diesel-mechanical locomotive, works no.22021, reverses a couple of wagons along the siding on 2nd February 2000. The bogie wagon behind the locomotive was originally built by MRCW as the undercarriage of guard brake third class passenger coach no.F44 in 1908. The body was scrapped in 1983. (T.Heavyside)

70.   A closer view of the stock hemmed in at the far end of the siding in the previous picture. Next to another bogie wagon is two-plank wagon no.M78, a product of MRCW in 1926. This was the last and 81st example of a design that first graced the island in 1877. Its pristine condition was the result of restoration work completed by the Isle of Man Railway Supporters Association in 1998. What appears to be Manx Electric Railway van no.8 was in fact a replica body constructed by the MER at their Derby Castle workshops in 1998 in order to camouflage a diesel generator. It was used on a number of occasions that year to propel MER car no.33 along the line to Port Erin as part of the IoMR 125th anniversary celebrations (see picture 100 in our *Douglas to Port Erin* album). (T.Heavyside)

71.   No.11 *Maitland* waits for the guard to give the 'right away' with the 14.00 (timetables using the 24 hour clock were first issued in 2000) to Port Erin on 26th April 2001. The coaching stock looks smart in the red and cream colour scheme (similar to that of earlier times) introduced the previous year. On the left, still in the previous standard dark purple lake livery, is 32-seater vestibule open third class coach no.F32, shipped across to the island from the MRCW factory in Birmingham in 1905. (T.Heavyside)

72.   Later that afternoon no.12 *Hutchinson* arrived with the 14.15 from Port Erin, and as passengers walk towards the exit the locomotive edges its way towards the buffer stops. Almost hidden by the palms, the fireman stands ready to throw over the point lever to allow *Hutchinson* to run round the coaching stock. It also gives an opportunity to view the station architecture on the opposite side of the building to that seen in picture 49, along with the single storey structure on the north side, part of which was once the porters room. In the centre of the frame the distinctive clock tower reaches skywards, although by way of contrast the backs of the properties on Peel Road do nothing to enhance the area. (T.Heavyside)

XI. The simplified layout at Douglas in 2017, following the alterations detailed in the earlier captions. Note the position of the 1998-erected carriage shed that can accommodate up to 16 coaches. The signal box was moved to the position annotated here the next year (see picture 73).

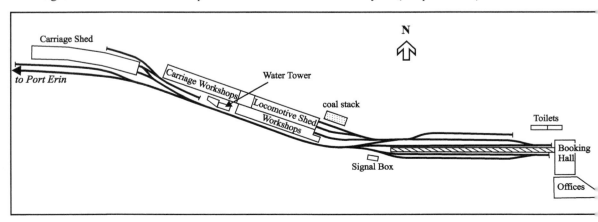

73.   On the rather dull evening of 8th August 2002 no.4 *Loch* leaves with a special to Santon. The redesign of the layout in 1982 left the signal box isolated from the running lines, but in January 1999 it was jacked-up and rolled across the yard to the position seen here. While the 36-lever frame remains in situ, the signals and points have not been reconnected. (T.Heavyside)

74.   No.8 *Fenella* departs with the 14.15 service for Castletown on 23rd October 2003. Isle of Man Transport double-decker buses await there next engagements in the area once occupied by platforms 5 and 6. (T.Heavyside)

75. No.13 *Kissack* prepares to go 'on shed' on 10th September 2006. The name bestowed on the engine is that of Edward Thomas Kissack who was elected a director of the IoMR in 1902. He served until 1927. In the background, by the double-decker bus, is the office block opened in 2000, the headquarters of Isle of Man Transport. The semaphore signals were erected in 2005. (T.Heavyside)

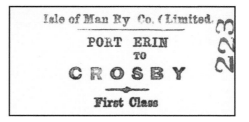

76.   One mile into its journey to Port Erin with the 4.10pm service from Douglas, no.12 *Hutchinson* approaches White Hoe Crossing on 6th May 1997. This ungated crossing formerly provided the means of access to a hospital (now closed); despite clear warning signs to motorists it witnessed a number of accidents over the years. However the installation of automatic controlled lifting barriers in 2007 has afforded better protection for all concerned. (T.Heavyside)

77. Working hard near Ellenbrook up the 1-in-65/70 climb towards Port Soderick is no.11 *Maitland* with the 11.45am Douglas to Port Erin service on 9th May 1997. The mountains in the background form part of the spectacular Northern Upland Massif, Snaefell being the highest peak at 2036ft above sea level. By far the easiest way to reach the summit is by boarding at Laxey one of the vintage overhead electric-powered cars that regularly ascend the steeply-graded 4¾-mile, 3ft 6in gauge Snaefell Mountain Railway. (T.Heavyside)

78. Near the summit of the line at Keristal, deputising at short notice for an ailing steam locomotive, no.17 *Viking* endeavours to make up a little lost time with the late running 11.45am service from Douglas on 18th July 1996. At this point passengers looking out of the windows on the south side of the train can enjoy a view over the Irish Sea beyond Port Soderick Bay. (T.Heavyside)

PORT SODERICK

79. The appropriate single line tokens are about to exchanged between the driver of no.12 *Hutchinson*, on a Castletown to Douglas service, and his colleague on no.5 *Mona* approaching from Douglas in July 1967. The station has been unstaffed since the late 1950s. In earlier years, especially on warm sunny days such as this, the platforms would have been thronged with day-trippers on their way to and from the nearby beach. The large building on the left, completed in 1896, included a licensed cafeteria to cater for their needs. There was accommodation for the station master on the first floor. Since 1984 it has been in private hands. (D.J.Mitchell)

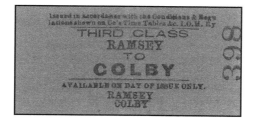

Issued in Accordance with the Conditions & Regu-
lations shown on Co's Time Tables &c. I.O.M. Ry
THIRD CLASS
RAMSEY
TO
COLBY
AVAILABLE ON DAY OF ISSUE ONLY.
RAMSEY
COLBY
398

80.   In contrasting liveries, nos 10 *G.H.Wood* and 12 *Hutchinson* call at this now quiet location before continuing to Douglas with the 4.15pm from Port Erin on 31st August 1993. The leading brake coach has a useful ducket lookout position for the guard, although there is little need for the luggage compartment these days. Note the double footboards to assist passengers when clambering in from ground level. (T.Heavyside)

81.   A second platform was added on the up side in 2003. The station has also been enhanced by the provision of smart waiting shelters and new running in boards. No.12 *Hutchinson* leaves for Port Erin on 23rd May 2015. (T.Heavyside)

SANTON

82.   The station was closed in 1958. Five years later no.13 *Kissack* scurries by this idyllic location with a mixed train of three coaches and three vans bound for Douglas during the summer of 1963. When the wooden building on the left was erected in 1875 it was intended only as a temporary expedient and over the years, due to inadequate foundations, developed a pronounced lean. Almost hidden, next to the building, is the body of former passenger brake van no.E2, built by MRCW in 1873. It was placed here in 1924 for use as a goods shed. Beyond are the remains of the hoardings that, in days gone by, concealed the siding so as to protect passengers from the sight and smell of quantities of horse manure, brought here by rail after being collected off the streets of Douglas. Some of the local farmers were glad of the supply. (D.Penney)

83.   The station was reopened as a 'request stop' in 1970. With no intending passengers in evidence no.15 *Caledonia* hurries by towards Port Erin on 17th July 1996. The palm trees are a distinctive feature. The hoardings were demolished in the late 1960s. (T.Heavyside)

84.   Two days later, no.10 *G.H.Wood* sets off bunker-first back to Douglas with a demonstration freight train. The narrow stone-faced bridge in the background supports the main A5 Douglas to Port Erin road. (T.Heavyside)

85.   Early in 2000 the building was restored to the perpendicular by lifting the rear some 3½in and underpinning with a more solid foundation. At the same time two platforms were laid and the track upgraded to allow passenger trains to use both lines. No.12 *Hutchinson* passes with the 16.20 from Douglas on 26th April 2001. Wagons loaded with lengths of rails occupy the siding on the right. (T.Heavyside)

BALLASALLA

86.   On a very pleasant day in July 1967 no.10 *G.H.Wood* halts while on its way to Castletown. A section of the wooden station building can be seen on the left. A couple of G vans rest in the siding reached via the connection with the up loop line. (D.J.Mitchell)

'Steam 125' postage stamps celebrating 125 years of Isle of Man Railways (1873-1998).

87.   In 1984 part of the goods yard was sold for redevelopment as commercial premises. Two years later a further plot was acquired by the developer, including where the wooden station building stood. It was replaced by a much more substantial structure, together with a platform on the down side. No.10 *G.H.Wood* prepares to restart the 10.50am from Douglas to Port Erin on 17th July 1996. Goods wagons again occupy the siding (T.Heavyside)

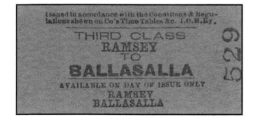

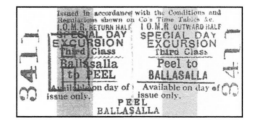

88. In recent years there has been a resurgence of interest in Manx Gaelic. In 2008 bilingual running in boards were erected at all stations except Colby (see picture 103), with the name written in both English and Manx. (T.Heavyside)

89. A platform was installed on the up side in 2001; it is now seldom used since as from the 2015 timetable regular services have been scheduled to cross at Castletown in preference to here. Having just passed over the A1 Douglas to Port Erin road, no.12 *Hutchinson* rolls past the large water tank with the 16.05 from Port Erin on 23rd May 2015. The facilities on the down platform can be appreciated, as can a Stevens & Son patent signal lever. (T.Heavyside)

RONALDSWAY HALT

90. This stopping place, close to the island's main airport, was opened in July 1967. The same month no.5 *Mona* approaches from Douglas. Facilities for passengers were non-existent but since spring 2003 intending passengers have benefited from a half-height platform. (D.J.Mitchell)

CASTLETOWN

91.   It is July 1967 and no.10 *G.H.Wood* has terminated with a train from Douglas. The surroundings at this the one-time capital of the island look decidedly neglected. The green-painted veranda had provided shelter since 1902; it once supported a decorative balustrade (see picture 76 in our *Douglas to Port Erin* album). (D.J.Mitchell)

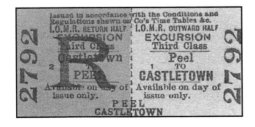

92.   A short-lived Ailsa initiative during the winter of 1967/68 was the introduction of a freight service to transport goods imported through Castletown harbour from Glasson Dock, Lancashire, to Douglas. The chassis from eleven former 'pairs' coaches assembled between 1912 and 1926, were adapted to carry containers and renumbered R1 to R11. Three of the empty container wagons, with no.R5 nearest the camera, stand idle along with two G vans at the back of the goods shed during the summer of 1968. On the right, gradually decaying in the undergrowth, are two of the surplus carriage bodies. Identifiable is no.F69, created in 1923 when the bodies of ex-nos B4 and B17 of 1873/74 vintage were mounted on a new underframe. All the discarded bodies were broken up later that year. (D.J.Mitchell)

93.   The veranda was removed in 1993 prior to work starting on a complete refurbishment of the station. No.11 *Maitland* is in charge of the 10.10am Douglas to Port Erin service on 17th July 1996. Access to Poulsom Park, behind the trees on the left, can be gained from the footpath that crosses the railway by the bridge in the background. (T.Heavyside)

94. Since 1998, passengers when boarding and alighting have enjoyed the convenience of platforms. Here, *Maitland* is on its way back to Douglas with the 12.05pm from Port Erin on 29th June 1999. (T.Heavyside)

95. No.7 *Tynwald* (the Manx Parliament) was the first of the Beyer Peacock 2-4-0Ts to be withdrawn in 1939, after registering 1,377,403 miles. For many years the dismantled remains stood on the loading dock outside the goods shed, as recorded in June 1999. In 2002 these remnants were moved to Port St Mary before being placed in store four years later. They were returned here in November 2009, but departed again in September 2012, this time to the fledgling Southwold Railway preservation scheme in Suffolk. What is left of no.7 is now housed at the Fengate Agricultural Light Railway, Weeting, Norfolk. Since 2012 the 1901-built goods shed has provided a work base for the Isle of Man Railway Supporters Association. (T.Heavyside)

96. On occasions, since the dawn of the Ailsa era in 1967, this has served as a terminal station. In 2002, buses substituted for trains between Santon and Castletown while a new sewer was laid beneath the trackbed. A young traveller looks in awe at no.12 *Hutchinson* as it awaits the arrival of a connecting bus, before leaving with the 15.30 to Port Erin on 18th May 2002. Since 1999 *Hutchinson* has had a similar appearance to its sisters, when at the conclusion of an overhaul a rounded cab and smaller side tanks were fitted (see picture 58). The former blue livery also gave way to a coat of Indian red. (T.Heavyside)

97. The next year the line from Santon was reopened, this then becoming the terminus for trains from Douglas while sewage work proceeded further west. No.8 *Fenella* takes water from the tank installed the previous year, before returning to the capital on 24th October 2003. (T.Heavyside)

WEST OF CASTLETOWN

98.   Shortly after leaving Castletown no.12 *Hutchinson*, hauling the 4.10pm from Douglas, receives an enthusiastic wave from the crossing-keeper at Mill Road on 20th July 1996. The gates are astride the A3 Castletown to St John's and Ramsey road, at its junction with the A5 Douglas to Port Erin road. The semaphore signal visible above the third coach is for the observance of Douglas-bound trains approaching Castletown station. The prominent road sign advises motorists to turn right at the roundabout for the town centre, or to bear left for Douglas and the airport. (T.Heavyside)

99.   The scene looking towards Port Erin at Mill Road in October 2003, when the railway was in possession of contractors undertaking sewage work. The notice on the gate clearly warns 'Danger Construction Site Keep Out'. Automatic lifting barriers and flashing lights now protect the crossing. (T.Heavyside)

BALLABEG

100. A short platform was laid and a veranda attached to the corrugated roofed platelayers hut at this 'request stop' in 1987. During the 1990s the site was embellished by a couple of milk churns and a number of old enamel advertising signs. Prominent were those advising to Insure with the Ocean and for Swan Vestas, the smoker's match. No.11 *Maitland* had no reason to stop while en route from Douglas to Port Erin on 9th May 1997. Since then the platform has been extended and a bilingual nameboard added, while in recent years members of the local Women's Institute have helped maintain the site. (T.Heavyside)

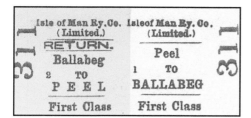

COLBY

101. The 'X' attached to the arm of this lower quadrant signal, located at the approach to the station from the east, indicates it was not in use. No.12 *Hutchinson* coasts past while in charge of the 4.10pm from Douglas on 6th May 1997. Gorse bushes add colour to the scene. Near this spot a level crossing, complete with automatic lifting barriers, has been installed to allow access to a new football ground. (T.Heavyside)

102. Following demolition of the original station building in 1978, waiting passengers had perforce to brave the elements. This was rectified in 1988 when the wooden structure previously at Braddan on the closed Peel line (see picture 5) was transported here. The nameboard was then attached to the roof. The doyen of the 2-4-0Ts no.1 *Sutherland* restarts the 16.15 Douglas to Port Erin service on 11th May 2000. The engine was named in honour of the third Duke of Sutherland, the first Chairman of the IoMR. Before being restored to service in 1998 the engine had been inactive since 1964, at which time it had completed over 1,480,000 miles. The boiler with bell-shaped dome and Ross 'pop' safety valves was borrowed from no.8 *Fenella*. (T.Heavyside)

103. After contractors had had charge of the site while laying new sewage pipes in 2003, the track was reinstated, platforms provided, and the area made to look much more presentable in time for the 2004 season. No.12 *Hutchinson* departing for Port Erin overtakes no.18 *Ailsa* on 24th September 2009. Note the new running in board in English only, this being the only station not to be adorned with a bilingual sign, there being no Manx equivalent of Colby. (T.Heavyside)

104. By walking along the up platform there was an opportunity to examine the four-wheeled diesel-hydraulic no.18 *Ailsa* at close quarters. Built as a 3ft 0in gauge locomotive by Hunslet-Barclay in 1990 for use on Channel Tunnel construction work, it was later modified to run on 2ft 0in gauge track to assist the London Underground Jubilee Line extension scheme. After reverting back to 3ft 0in gauge it was brought to the island by contractors undertaking track relaying after completion of the sewage work between Santon and Port St Mary. It was later purchased by the IoMR. The red and yellow warning plates look as if they may have been intended for the back of a lorry! The tractor on the well-wagon is used for lineside hedge cutting, while the rear wagon carries a couple of water tanks which are available for fire duty in case of need. The underframe of the latter was originally built by MRCW in 1922 to form the chassis of 'pairs' coach no.F70, but in 2000 the old bodies were dismantled and the frame adapted to support a new ballast hopper wagon before being used as seen here. More recently it has again been utilised as a ballast wagon to support work being undertaken on the Manx Electric Railway. (T.Heavyside)

THE LEVEL

105. Half-a-mile beyond Colby is this request stop by the B33 road. Also referred to over the years as plain Level and Colby Level, it must be one of the shortest platforms anywhere! This was the view from the roadway looking towards Douglas on 23rd May 2015. The building was previously the preserve of the gatekeeper, his services having been replaced by automation. (T.Heavyside)

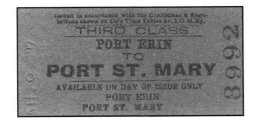

PORT ST MARY

106. As the guard scrambles into his compartment at the rear of the train, no.16 *Mannin* makes a spirited departure, on the last stage of its journey to Port Erin in July 1963. Coupled behind the bunker of *Mannin* is brake third no.F48 built in 1923 by MRCW. At the far end of the platform an IoMR lorry also looks set to leave. Stabled in the siding nearest the running line are an M wagon and a G van. (D.Penney)

107. Nos 11 *Maitland* and 10 *G.H.Wood* prepare to continue their journey with the 2.10pm from Douglas on 19th July 1996. An array of vintage tractors are on display in front of the goods shed, the two former sidings having been lifted, although one was relaid in 2003. (T.Heavyside)

108. No.12 *Hutchinson* delays traffic on Station Road while departing towards Castletown on 9th August 2002. The cars on the left are heading away from the town centre and harbour areas. The leading brake third no.F45 was imported from MRCW in 1913. In 1927 two of the five compartments were redesigned as first class, identifiable by '1' painted on the door panels. On this warm day four droplight windows have been opened for extra ventilation. Today the former crossing-keepers cottage on the right is privately owned. (T.Heavyside)

PORT ERIN

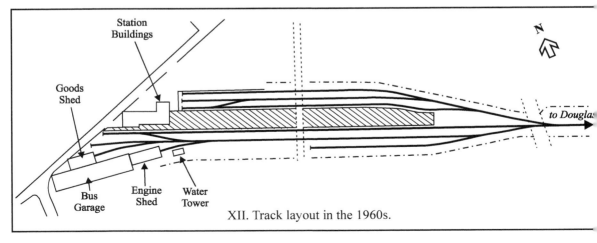

XII. Track layout in the 1960s.

109. The commodious, well-appointed red brick building was completed in 1905. The railcars had not long arrived from Douglas on a very pleasant afternoon in June 1968. (D.J.Mitchell)

> **Other views along this beautiful line to the south of the island can be seen in our _Douglas to Port Erin_ album.**

110. Both platforms were occupied during a visit in September 1974. No.11 _Maitland_ heads a train at the main platform as no.13 _Kissack_ does likewise at the shorter bay on the right. The line on the left provided access to the engine and goods sheds as well as serving as a run round loop. The break in the platform marks the public footpath that links Station Road and Athol Park. The shop premises in the background are on the opposite side of Station Road. (D.J.Mitchell)

111. In 1983 the goods shed was adapted as the engine shed. Having rested overnight no.12 *Hutchinson* stands outside on 17th July 1996. The blue waters of Port Erin Bay can be glimpsed beyond the traffic signals on Station Road. (T.Heavyside)

112. Later the same morning *Hutchinson* noisily leaves with the 10.15am to Douglas. Again no.F45 is the leading coach (see picture 108), but then painted like the rest of the stock in the earlier garb of dark purple lake. A single-deck bus takes up space on the platform. In the background, overlooking the bay, is the distinctive Milner's Tower on Bradda Head. (T.Heavyside)

XIII. The revised layout from 1998. Note the old goods shed, after being revamped for a second time, now serving as an entrance area to the museum. The new carriage facility was provided in 1998.

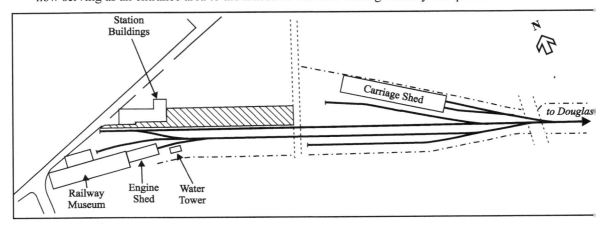

113. As three young steam enthusiasts soak up the atmosphere, long-serving driver John Elkin, oilcan in hand, walks purposely past no.9 *Douglas* basking in the sunshine on 19th July 1996. Withdrawn from service in November 1953, *Douglas* is worthy of study in that it still has an original style sloping smokebox front, a bell-shaped dome and Salter safety valves. The boiler was fitted in 1912. During the mid-1990s *Douglas* was normally confined to the old engine shed as part of the museum collection. Behind *Douglas* are nos 10 *G.H.Wood* and 11 *Maitland*. (T.Heavyside)

114. Having deposited the stock forming the last arrival of the day from Douglas in the carriage shed, completed the previous autumn, no.15 *Caledonia* reverses slowly over Droghadfayle Road on 29th June 1999. The crossing-keepers hut is on the right. The traditional gates have since been replaced by automatic lifting barriers. (T.Heavyside)

115. A Stevens & Son of London & Glasgow signal lever located on the east side of Droghadfayle Road. The semaphore signal to be observed by trains approaching from the capital normally works automatically but the Stevens lever remains connected in case of need. A similar lever is exhibited in the nearby museum. (T.Heavyside)

116. In August 1997, after experiencing a more sanitised existence for some 14 years as part of the museum complex (the taller building behind), the old engine shed resumed its original purpose. The following year, a stone tower was erected to support the water tank, on the same site as the original one. No.12 *Hutchinson* reposes outside on 9th August 2002. (T.Heavyside)

117. In 2003, while sewage work progressed west of Castletown, a steam presence was maintained by a shuttle service to and from Port St Mary. On 24th October of that year, looking smart in a coat of deep blue paint with red lining, no.15 *Caledonia* had charge of a single coach, brake third no.F26 built in 1896 by MRCW. The engine has since been returned to its more traditional Manx Northern livery. A couple of ladies head for the tea room housed in the west wing of the building. (T.Heavyside)

118. The doors of the two-road carriage shed were open on 10th September 2006. It can accommodate up to ten carriages. Just inside is Motor-Rail four-wheeled diesel-mechanical no.22021, used as the station pilot. The redundant water column was a product of Ransomes & Rapier Ltd of Ipswich. (T.Heavyside)

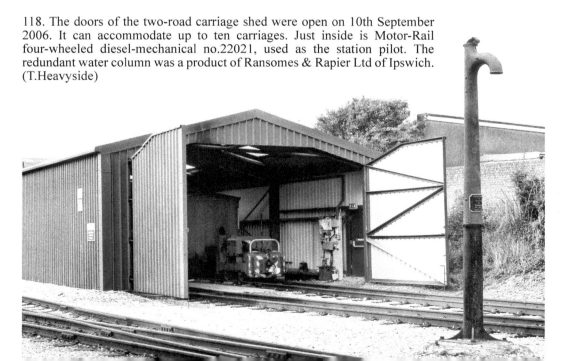

Port Erin Railway Museum

In 1975 the vacated bus garage, adjacent to the station, was converted into a railway museum. In 1983 when the old goods shed became the engine shed, the previous locomotive facility was incorporated into the museum. During a major refurbishment in 1997 and early 1998 the former goods/engine shed was redesigned as an entrance hall and shop, with access gained either direct from the station platform or Station Road. Over the years a number of out-of-service locomotives (listed in the accompanying table) and carriages have been displayed, while an interesting array of smaller items, including sections devoted to the workshops, signalling and permanent way, help visitors interpret the history of the island's railways.

Locomotives Displayed in the Museum

No.	Name	From	To
1	*Sutherland*	1975	1996
4	*Loch*	1998	2000
6	*Peveril*	2000	Date
9	*Douglas*	1993	1997
15	*Caledonia*	1975	1993
16	*Mannin*	1975	Date

119. Comfortably settled in the museum in July 1996 is no.1 *Sutherland*. It is in the preferred colours of Lord Ailsa as applied in the late 1960s. A snowplough, seldom needed on the island, sits in front of the engine. The walls are bedecked with various historic artefacts and sundry information boards. On the right is the doorway to the annexed shed building, then an integral part of the museum. (T.Heavyside)

120. With a level crossing gate seemingly barring its way no.16 *Mannin* is seen at rest in May 2015. On the left is no.F36 'The Queen's Coach', so called following its use as the Royal Saloon on the visit of the Queen Mother in 1963. Just visible is no.6 *Peveril* while a number of enamel signs decorate the far wall. Among the myriad exhibits is a mock-up of a booking office desk complete with ledgers. An old booking office board, out of sight behind *Mannin*, serves as a timely reminder to 'haste ye back' to this enchanting island. (T.Heavyside)

Isle of Man Railways postage stamps (May 2013)

MP Middleton Press

EVOLVING THE ULTIMATE RAIL ENCYCLOPEDIA

Easebourne Midhurst GU29 9AZ. Tel:01730 813169

www.middletonpress.co.uk   email:info@middletonpress.co.uk

A-978 0 906520 B- 978 1 873793 C- 978 1 901706 D-978 1 904474
E - 978 1 908108 F - 978 1 908174 G - 978 1 910356